Gaming and eSports

POWER ON

THE HISTORY OF GAMING

Kaitlyn Duling

D1297930

Rourke
Educational Media

A Division of
Carson
Dellosa
Education.

Before Reading: *Building Background Knowledge and Vocabulary*

Building background knowledge can help children process new information and build upon what they already know. Before reading a book, it is important to tap into what children already know about the topic. This will help them develop their vocabulary and increase their reading comprehension.

Questions and Activities to Build Background Knowledge:

1. Look at the front cover of the book and read the title. What do you think this book will be about?
2. What do you already know about this topic?
3. Take a book walk and skim the pages. Look at the table of contents, photographs, captions, and bold words. Did these text features give you any information or help you predict what you will read in this book?

Vocabulary: *Vocabulary Is Key to Reading Comprehension*

Use the following directions to prompt a conversation about each word.

- Read the vocabulary words.
- What comes to mind when you see each word?
- What do you think each word means?

Vocabulary Words:
- cartridge
- consoles
- developers
- gamepads
- mobile gaming
- programmers

During Reading: *Reading for Meaning and Understanding*

To achieve deep comprehension of a book, children are encouraged to use close reading strategies. During reading, it is important to have children stop and make connections. These connections result in deeper analysis and understanding of a book.

 Close Reading a Text

During reading, have children stop and talk about the following:

- Any confusing parts
- Any unknown words
- Text to text, text to self, text to world connections
- The main idea in each chapter or heading

Encourage children to use context clues to determine the meaning of any unknown words. These strategies will help children learn to analyze the text more thoroughly as they read.

When you are finished reading this book, turn to the next-to-last page for After Reading Questions and an Activity.

Table of Contents

BLAST TO THE PAST

You know how it feels when you win a game? Zoom across the finish line? Beat the high score? Gamers have been chasing that winning feeling for decades. The earliest video games look nothing like today's mega-battles and virtual worlds. But without them, we wouldn't have the characters, stories, and competitions we love.

Let's travel back in time to see how video games got their start. Think you can get a high score in video game history?

Game on!

MOMENTS IN HISTORY

Nimatron	Tennis For Two	Computer Space
1940	1958	1971

SHALL

WE PLAY A

GAME?

GH SCORE: 19832323.............WOPR

Pac-Man

Pokémon

Nintendo Wii

1980

1996

2006

Hold on tight. We're traveling back in time. To learn the history of video games, you have to start with computers. They didn't exist until the 1940s. The first computers were huge. They filled entire rooms! Computer **programmers** created games to test the potential of these new machines. The first computer games were very simple, like tic-tac-toe.

PROGRAMMERS (PROH-gram-ers):
people who create computer programs, including games

The Harvard University mainframe Mark I
in Cambridge, Massachusetts, was built by IBM.

SPORTS ON THE SCREEN

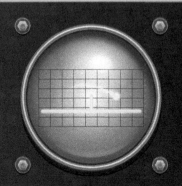

The very first video game was
created in 1958. Physicist William
Higinbotham spent two weeks
building *Tennis for Two*. Players used
a knob and a button. They hit a ball
back and forth on the screen.

While programmers built new games, there were other ways to play. Pinball machines were introduced in the 1930s. The machines use flippers to hit a small metal ball and score points. They offered a cheap form of fun during the Great Depression. Pinball machines are still played today. The world record for the longest pinball game is 32 hours straight!

A FAIR GAME

Another early game machine was the Nimatron. It was first displayed in April 1940 at the 1939 New York World's Fair. Users played against the machine in a math game called Nim. At the fair, Nimatron won 90,000 out of 100,000 games played!

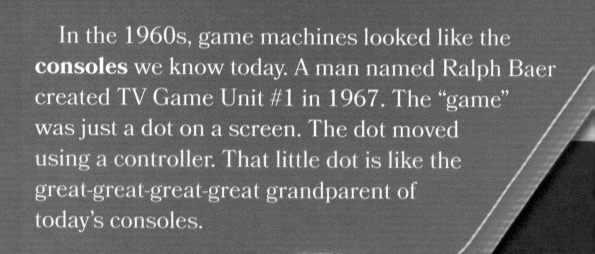

In the 1960s, game machines looked like the **consoles** we know today. A man named Ralph Baer created TV Game Unit #1 in 1967. The "game" was just a dot on a screen. The dot moved using a controller. That little dot is like the great-great-great-great grandparent of today's consoles.

Baer (right) is considered the father of the home video game console.

CONSOLES (KAHN-soles):

electronic systems that connect to a display (such as a TV or monitor) and are used primarily to play video games

GOLDEN AGE OF ARCADE GAMES

Got a quarter? In the 1970s and 1980s, quarters came in handy. That is, if you wanted to play games. This time period was the golden age of arcades. Instead of playing at home, gamers went to arcades. There, they could find their favorite characters, such as Pac-Man and Donkey Kong. *Computer Space* was the first widely played arcade video game. It was released in 1971.

ONE PLUMBER'S SUPER ORIGINS

Before he became the Mario we know today, this famous character was an unnamed carpenter. He first appeared in 1981's *Donkey Kong* arcade game. He was known as "Jumpman."

"Mario" was named after landlord Mario Segale who rented a warehouse to Nintendo.

Some of the earliest video games are still very popular. *Tetris* is one of the most successful of all time! It was based on a wooden block puzzle. The video game was created in 1984 by Alexey Pajitnov, a Russian engineer. In 1988, it was released in arcades. Since 2010, the Classic Tetris World Championship tournament has been held in Portland, Oregon.

INVADING ARCADES

In 1978, *Space Invaders* was introduced in Japan. It became so popular that it caused a country wide shortage of 100-yen coins!

A year later, there were 6,000 *Space Invaders* machines across the United States.

PONG

IS THE

BIRTH

OF THE

HOME

CONSOLE.

One of history's most famous video games is *Pong*. In *Pong*, players bounce a ball back and forth. That's it! The first machine was added to an arcade in 1972. After a while, the game stopped working. The owners thought it had broken, but it was just jammed with coins!

THE
END TO
ARCADES
BEGINS.
GAME
OVER.

In 1975, a home version of *Pong* came out. Players didn't have to go to arcades anymore. They could play *Pong* from the comfort of their living rooms. Arcades remained popular throughout the 80s, but people eventually tired of them. In the 1990s, video games came home to stay.

HOME SWEET HOME

Remember Ralph Baer? After TV Game Unit #1, Baer kept thinking and working. He came up with the Brown Box. It had two controllers and several games. Users could play checkers, ping-pong, and even target shooting. Magnavox bought Baer's Brown Box. Renamed the Magnavox Odyssey, it was released in 1972. It was the very first home video console.

The Brown Box

The Odyssey

1972

The Brown Box was the first of its kind, but 1977's Atari 2600 was the first console to be a hit. Atari had a joystick that players used for over 100 different games. Each game existed on a **cartridge**. Though it might sound normal now, having games that could be switched out on the same console was an entirely new idea.

In 1985, Nintendo released its own system, the NES. Nintendo originally started as a playing card company in 1889. The company is responsible for many popular consoles and video games. They created legends like Mario, Kirby, Link, and more!

GIRLS IN GAMES

The number and variety of video games exploded in the 1980s. Girls and boys of all ages loved to play, but there was one problem. There were no female video game characters in the U.S.! Finally, in 1986, Nintendo introduced Samus Aran, the star of the *Metroid* games. Samus Aran is remembered as one of the first female video game characters.

(NES) Nintendo Entertainment System

CARTRIDGE (KAHR-trij): a case for holding printed circuit chips containing a computer program

In the 1980s and 1990s, video games evolved. **Gamepads** replaced joysticks. And the games themselves were getting more complex. In 1987 a groundbreaking Japanese video game called *Final Fantasy* was released. This was one of the first popular role-playing games, or RPGs.

Final Fantasy first launched on the NES.

Along with new games, this time period brought new ways to play. In 1989, Nintendo introduced the Game Boy. This handheld console changed how people played. People could take games on the road.

MAJOR FAIL

In 1982, Atari released a video game called *E.T. the Extra-Terrestrial*. It was based on a popular movie, but the game was a total flop! Some say it is the worst video game of all time. Instead of destroying all the extra games, Atari secretly buried almost a million cartridges in the New Mexico desert.

Cartridges were recovered from the landfill on April 26, 2014.

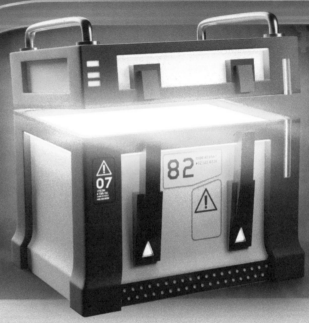

Video games have been evolving for decades. Possibly the biggest change? The internet. By the 1990s, gamers could play online. Websites hosted their own simple games. Those would eventually become the massively multiplayer online games, or MMOs, we know today. The internet allowed people to connect, communicate, and play with gamers all over the world.

The original PlayStation debuted in 1994. This console was one of the first to use disks. The flat disks held much more memory than cartridges. This made room for **developers** to create longer, more advanced video games. Graphics got better and better. Today's games look more like 3D cartoons than they do their pixelated ancestors.

Black PS1 Disc

DEVELOPERS (dih-VEL-uh-perz):
people who create computer software, such as video games

The late 1990s and early 2000s brought even more creativity to the video game world. *Dance Dance Revolution* got gamers on their feet. *Rock Band* and *Guitar Hero* had instrument-shaped controllers. And in 2006, the Wii transformed the way sports could be played on a game console.

The Nintendo Wii released in 2006 and used motion to play.

Guest F
Record 15 pts

Many of today's most popular video games are played online. Games such as *Call of Duty*, *Among Us*, and *Dota 2* allow players to battle with people from around the world in realtime. Thanks to the internet, **mobile gaming** has spread fast. Smartphones and tablets have become the console-of-choice for many casual gamers.

It's hard to believe, but we wouldn't have today's games without pinball, *Tennis for Two*, and other early inventions. If we've come this far in less than a century, where could games go next? When it comes to video games, the only limit is our imaginations.

MOBILE GAMING (MOH-buhl GAY-ming):
gaming that uses a smartphone or tablet to play

MEMORY GAME

Look at the pictures. What do you remember
reading on the pages where each image appeared?

INDEX

AFTER-READING QUESTIONS

1. Why were the first computer games created?

2. What are three famous games created before 1990?

3. How did the internet change the way people played video games?

4. What made pinball such a popular game?

5. How have game controllers evolved over time?

ACTIVITY

Think back to the games and consoles discussed in the book. Choose some of your favorite highlights from video game history to include in a short timeline. List the events in chronological order—from oldest to most recent. Get creative! Draw pictures or use paper and glue to make your timeline unique.

ABOUT THE AUTHOR

Kaitlyn Duling is a lifelong lover of video games. She enjoys games that get her moving, thinking, and dreaming. When she's not on her Nintendo Switch, Kaitlyn is writing and living in Washington, DC. She has authored over 100 books for kids and teens.

www.rourkeeducationalmedia.com

PHOTO CREDITS ©: page 4: Inked Pixels/Shutterstock.com; page 6: akg-images/Newscom; page 6: Everett Collection/Newscom; page 7: akg-images/Newscom; page 8: Ed Oudenaarden/ANP/Newscom; page 10: Jens Wolf/dpa/picture-alliance/Newscom; page 12: Britta Pedersen/dpa/picture-alliance/Newscom; page 12: Atmosphere1 / Shutterstock.com; page 12: Thanaphat Kingkaew/ Shutterstock.com; page 12: Atmosphere1/ Shutterstock.com; page 13: Sean Locke Photography/ Shutterstock.com; page 13: Alternative Publicidad/ Shutterstock.com; page 13: Karl Polverino/ZUMA Press/Newscom; page 14: Thomas Eisenhuth/dpa/picture-alliance/Newscom; page 14: yavdat/ Getty Images; page 15: PERCY RAMIREZ/EL COMERCIO de PERU/Newscom; page 15: MicroOne/ Shutterstock.com; page 18: SK2/HS1/Stefan Krempl / WENN/Newscom; page 19: Taner Muhlis Karaguzel / Shutterstock.com; page 19: Jovanmandic/ Getty Images; page 19: Spiderstock/ Getty Images; page 20: JR Moreira / Shutterstock.com; page 21: robtek / Shutterstock.com; page 21: seeshooteatrepeat/ Shutterstock.com; page 21: robtek / Shutterstock.com; page 22: rambo182/ Shutterstock.com; page 22: Matthieu Tuffet / Shutterstock.com; page 22: Sushiman / Shutterstock.com; page 22: Jorge Gonzalez/ ZUMA Press/Newscom; page 23: igorrita/ Shutterstock.com; page 23: MARK WILSON/REUTERS/Newscom; page 24: solarseven/ Getty Images; page 24: photo_Pawel/ Getty Images; page 25: robtek / Shutterstock.com; page 25: Yuliia Markova/ Shutterstock.com; page 26: ia2ca/ Shutterstock.com; page 26: withGod / Shutterstock.com; page 27: Andrew Parsons GDA Photo Service/Newscom; page 27: seeshooteatrepeat / Shutterstock.com; page 27: Splash News/Newscom; page 28: robtek / Shutterstock.com; page 28: Artos/ Shutterstock.com; page 29: Wachiwit / Shutterstock.com; page 29: F-Stop boy / Shutterstock.com; page 29: babysofja/ Shutterstock.com; page n/a: amtitus/ Getty Images; n/a: amtitus/ Getty Images

Edited by: Jennifer Doyle
Cover design and illustration by: Joshua Janes
Interior design and illustrations by: Joshua Janes

Library of Congress PCN Data

Power On The History Of Gaming / Kaitlyn Duling
(Gaming and eSports)
ISBN 978-1-73164-891-4 (hard cover)
ISBN 978-1-73164-839-6 (soft cover)
ISBN 978-1-73164-943-0 (e-Book)
ISBN 978-1-73164-995-9 (e-Pub)
Library of Congress Control Number: 2021935281

Rourke Educational Media
Printed in the United States of America
02-09422119570

CPSIA information can be obtained
at www.ICGtesting.com
Printed in the USA
BVHW061304010422
633121BV00001B/5